American Symbols
AND THEIR Meanings

MOUNT
RUSHMORE

American Symbols AND THEIR Meanings

MOUNT RUSHMORE

LAURA HAHN

MASON CREST PUBLISHERS
PHILADELPHIA

Produced by OTTN Publishing, Stockton, N.J.

Mason Crest Publishers
370 Reed Road
Broomall PA 19008
www.masoncrest.com

3 5 7 9 8 6 4 2

Library of Congress Cataloging-in-Publication Data

Hahn, Laura.
   Mount Rushmore / Laura Hahn.
       p. cm. — (American symbols and their meanings)
Summary: Discusses the history and construction of South Dakota's Mount Rushmore, and provides facts about the four presidents represented there: Washington, Jefferson, Lincoln, and Theodore Roosevelt.
   Includes bibliographical references and index.
   ISBN 1-59084-027-5
1. Mount Rushmore National Memorial (S.D.)—Juvenile literature.
[1. Mount Rushmore National Memorial (S.D.) 2. National monuments.]
I. Title. II. Series.
F657.R8H34 2003
978.3'93—dc21

                                                        2002009582

Publisher's note: all quotations in this book come from original sources, and contain the spelling and grammatical inconsistencies of the original text.

American Symbols
AND THEIR Meanings

CONTENTS

THE IMPORTANCE OF AMERICAN SYMBOLS

Symbols are not merely ornaments to admire—they also tell us stories. If you look at one of them closely, you may want to find out why it was made and what it truly means. If you ask people who live in the society in which the symbol exists, you will learn some things. But by studying the people who created that symbol and the reasons why they made it, you will understand the deepest meanings of that symbol.

The United States owes its identity to great events in history, and the most remarkable American Symbols are rooted in these events. The struggle for independence from Great Britain gave America the Declaration of Independence, the Liberty Bell, the American flag, and other images of freedom. The War of 1812 gave the young country a song dedicated to the flag, "The Star-Spangled Banner," which became our national anthem. Nature gave the country its national animal, the bald eagle. These symbols established the identity of the new nation, and set it apart from the nations of the Old World.

To be emotionally moving, a symbol must strike people with a sense of power and unity. But it often takes a long time for a new symbol to be accepted by all the people, especially if there are older symbols that have gradually lost popularity. For example, the image of Uncle Sam has replaced Brother Jonathan, an earlier representation of the national will, while the Statue of Liberty has replaced Columbia, a woman who represented liberty to Americans in the early 19th century. Since then, Uncle Sam and the Statue of Liberty have endured and have become cherished icons of America.

Of all the symbols, the Statue of Liberty has perhaps the most curious story, for unlike other symbols, Americans did not create her. She was created by the French, who then gave her to America. Hence, she represented not what Americans thought of their country but rather what the French thought of America. It was many years before Americans decided to accept this French goddess of Liberty as a symbol for the United States and its special role among the nations: to spread freedom and enlighten the world.

This series of books is valuable because it presents the story of each of America's great symbols in a freshly written way and will contribute to the students' knowledge and awareness of them. It is to be hoped that this information will awaken an abiding interest in American history, as well as in the meanings of American symbols.

—*Barry Moreno,*
librarian and historian
Ellis Island/Statue of Liberty National Monument

The image of Confederate generals begins to emerge from the granite face of Stone Mountain. Sculptor Gutzon Borglum was working on this project when he was invited to South Dakota to take on another task: carving the heads of four of America's greatest presidents onto Mount Rushmore.

WHERE DREAMS BEGIN

*W*here does a grand scheme begin? What prompts the building of towers and monuments, dams and castles, cathedrals and temples that pepper the entire earth, on every continent? There is only one place where that can begin: in the mind and heart of the human being. Animals don't build large monuments or construct their image in art. Mother Nature submits no business plan for its international growth and development. Only man builds on such a large scale and for reasons beyond the basic need of food, shelter, and clothing. Only man builds monuments to reflect a spirit, an ideal, or a dream. And only man

How do you get a mountain named after you? When the young lawyer, Charles E. Rushmore, was sent to South Dakota in 1885 to investigate mining opportunities for a client, he got to know some locals, who came to like him. While on a horseback ride through the hills, he asked about a mountain's name. The locals generously named it after him.

does so to serve as a reminder to present and future generations of the values held dear by the people who constructed the monument.

Mount Rushmore, a gigantic sculpture of four American presidents carved into a mountain of granite in the Black Hills of South Dakota, is a prime example of such a monument. While there is no doubt that the monument itself is awe-inspiring, the story of how that grand dream was born, developed, worked, and realized is even more amazing.

As is true with many grand projects, the way Mount Rushmore looks today was not the original proposal. The idea began with an aging man who loved history and his home state of South Dakota. As he reached his mid-60s, Doane Robinson probably reflected on his life and what he valued when he came up with an idea to help his home state. That was in 1923. The country was in a boom time, with lots of industry and inventions occurring. Skyscrapers were being built, automobiles were being *mass-produced*, and the ideas for TV, 16-mm movie cameras, "talkie" movies, and the videodisc were all emerging. *Prosperity* abounded and people had the time, money, and cars to travel around the country.

As founder and superintendent of the South Dakota Historical Society, Robinson believed that more people should visit his beautiful state. South Dakota had been the home of Wild West characters and powerful Indian tribes. It had been the site of gold mines and important battles. To attract visitors, Robinson believed South Dakota needed something special to make it a destination for travelers.

While much of South Dakota is flat, rising up from its prairies on the western side of the state are the magical Black Hills. Dark, mysterious, and sacred to the Native Americans, these hills begin the mountain region of the United States. They are so old, no one knows for sure when they were formed.

Within the Black Hills are massive mountains of granite. One area called the Needles is a cluster of tall, thin spires of granite poking into the sky. Doane Robinson thought they could be carved into towering images of the romantic western frontier heroes. He envisioned a parade of American explor-

The Teton Sioux tribe called the Black Hills "Paha Sapa." For the Native Americans it was a sacred place used only for ceremonies. The land was reserved as a resting spot for the spirits of their dead warriors, so that their eyes would become accustomed to beauty before they entered into paradise. Young warriors were also sent to the hills to seek Wakan Tanka, the Great Spirit, who would guide their futures.

The area of the Black Hills known as the Needles consists of tall spires of granite, which have been worn down through years of erosion by wind and weather. Doane Robinson originally envisioned carvings of American heroes on these spires.

ers such as Buffalo Bill, Lewis and Clark, and Sioux warriors such as Sitting Bull or Crazy Horse. He thought it could be a sculptural gateway to the west, a prelude to the Rocky Mountains that would put South Dakota on the must-see map for travelers.

Robinson was not the first to have such a grand imagination. Twenty-seven years earlier, the Statue of Liberty was unveiled, rising 300 feet above New York Harbor. And nearly 75 years earlier, a Missouri Senator had proposed a large carving of Christopher Columbus in the Rockies. The idea of making enormous sculptures had become especially popular since the turn of the century. Larger-than-life memorials, statues, and sculptures were *commissioned* by the government, religious groups, and private investors to adorn and commemorate public and private buildings, parks, and spaces. And at the very same time when Doane Robinson was conceiving his dream, there was already someone carving a mountain in Georgia in the image of General Robert E. Lee and other Confederate generals. That someone was sculptor Gutzon Borglum.

Ideas and dreams are fleeting things which, when shared, can grow into something else, something bigger. When Doane Robinson shared his idea with other leaders, such as South Dakota Senator Peter Norbeck and state representative William Williamson, he found great support. They agreed it would be great for South Dakota to have such a monument, and they began to seek a sculptor who could make that dream into a reality. Their search ultimately led to Borglum who, in the midst of having trouble with the mountain carving committee in Georgia, enthusiastically responded to their request to come and see the Needles in South Dakota.

This photo shows how Mount Rushmore appeared in the mid-1920s, when Gutzon Borglum first saw the mountain. The sculptor decided this granite mountain would be the perfect place for his colossal sculpture.

MAKING THE DIFFERENCE

*W*hen Gutzon Borglum arrived in the Black Hills in 1924 to study the proposal, he made his opinion known. Traveling into the hills to see the Needles on horseback with his son and a guide, Borglum immediately asserted his intense and commanding personality. First, he declared the Needles location unsuitable. The stone was too brittle for carving and the spires were not the right shape for the human figure. Second, he did not want to immortalize regional heroes. Being the son of immigrant parents who raised him in the wilds of the developing west, he had great passion for the spirit of America. He wanted this project, because of its gigantic size, to reflect a vision that embodied the gigantic ideals of this great nation. Borglum said:

> A monument's dimension should be determined by the importance to civilization of the events commemorated. We are . . . setting down a few crucial . . . facts regarding the accomplishments of the Old World radicals . . . who built an empire and rewrote the philosophy of freedom and compelled the world to accept its wiser, happier forms of government.

Borglum was as passionate about his patriotism as he was about his sculpture. At the end of his first visit he wrote an impassioned letter outlining the inappropriateness of the Needles location along with his enthusiasm for the project. He wrote energetically about his desire to carve a memorial so high up that it would be protected from vandalism. And he believed that this project should rightfully be located in the heart of the great country he so loved.

A year later, in September 1925, Borglum returned with his son Lincoln and assistant Major Tucker. They joined the state forester, Theodore Shoemaker, on a search through the Harney

Sculpting a mountain was something Gutzon Borglum had never done prior to Stone Mountain, Georgia. And even then, he didn't know to use dynamite until a Belgian engineer, visiting America, dropped by Stone Mountain to see what was going on. He shared with Gutzon his use of dynamite to clear tunnel passages when building roads. Soon a new sculpting technique was born.

John Gutzon de la Mothe Borglum was born in St. Charles, Idaho, on March 25, 1867, to Danish Mormons. At an early age he showed a talent for sketching. After college he moved to California, established a studio, and began selling paintings in his early 20s. He traveled to Paris to further his studies in painting and discovered he loved sculpting.

He achieved moderate fame through his carving of the Saints and Apostles for the Cathedral of St John the Divine in New York City, the seated Lincoln in Newark, New Jersey, the oversized Lincoln bust for the U.S. Capitol and at Lincoln's tomb in Springfield, Illinois, as well as other works.

As Borglum's sculpting career grew, so did his desire to work on a large scale. That dream was realized in 1915 when the United Daughters of the Confederacy asked him to carve General Robert E. Lee on Stone Mountain in Georgia. World War I delayed the work, but carving began in 1923. The work on Stone Mountain led to the Mount Rushmore commission. While still working on Rushmore he also contributed to a plan to carve the Indian Chief Crazy Horse on another mountain in the Black Hills. He died in Chicago at age 74 and is buried in a crypt at the foot of Mount Rushmore.

Mountain range to find a suitable setting for the grand vision in the sculptor's mind. Climbing Harney Peak, the highest peak between the Rocky Mountains and the Swiss Alps, Borglum saw a panorama of pine trees, rolling in the breeze, making a waving emerald carpet in the sky. From Harney Peak, he could see 17 other peaks with great bare granite tops. Directly across, he spied Mount Rushmore. This site had everything Borglum desired. It was smooth-grained granite, strong enough to carve. It was relatively free from fracture, which would give Borglum a surface that would probably not weaken and break apart over time. It was 5,700 feet in the air, dominating the surrounding terrain and not easily accessible, a plus for preventing vandalism. And its southeastern side faced the sun most of the day. This provided the longest and best illumination for viewing the finished sculpture.

When Gutzon Borglum made up his mind about anything, there was little that could be done to change it. So even though powerful Senator Norbeck was disappointed with the remote location, based on the fact that there were no roads—much less wagon trails—to the mountain, Borglum would have his way. Doane Robinson, on the other hand, was very happy. Even though his

> **Building Iron Mountain Road, which leads up to Mount Rushmore, was a feat in itself because Senator Norbeck wanted a truly scenic road. The engineers thought he was crazy to insist on going over and through the mountain and said so. Norbeck insisted, claiming that engineers didn't know a park from a ranch when it came to scenery. In the end everyone was very happy with the completion of a scenic road featuring three tunnels that provide spectacular views of Mount Rushmore in the distance.**

At age 26 in the summer of 1939, Glenn Bradford worked on Mount Rushmore. He worked primarily on the mustache and chin of Roosevelt. During his time he met Gutzon Borglum and found him to be eccentric and demanding. "You had to do things his way. Even though another person made suggestions, Borglum would twist it around so it was his idea," said Bradford. "Everybody tried to keep out of his way so they wouldn't get fired."

original concept may have been changed, he could see that the essence of his dream—a tourist attraction—could become a reality in the hands of such a passionate sculptor and champion. With the contract for the sculptor secured, Robinson was confident that the small matter of bringing people to the location could surely be overcome.

The four presidents pictured on Mount Rushmore—George Washington, Thomas Jefferson, Abraham Lincoln, and Theodore Roosevelt—were selected because of their importance in American history. Each represents a different aspect of American life.

DESIGNING THE DREAM

*B*efore becoming a sculptor, Gutzon Borglum had been a successful painter. He made his living painting portraits, murals, and other commissions. When he traveled to Europe looking for new clients, he became exposed to sculpture. Auguste Rodin, a famous French sculptor of that time, greatly influenced Borglum. The size and three-dimensional aspect of sculpture fired Borglum's soul. By 1901, Borglum had given up painting to create sculptures full-time.

Having become a sculptor after a successful career as a painter, Borglum's artistic visions were often made up of multiple figures. These factors naturally influenced his decision-making on the yet-to-be-determined Mount Rushmore monument.

But before he started planning the monument, Borglum declared that the first order of business was to have a dedication ceremony to mark the start of the project. Borglum understood the value of promotion, and used it to gain support for his art. His charm and sense of drama kept him in the newspapers and in the minds of the people he wanted to attract and persuade. In October 1925, just a month after selecting the site, he staged the first of many Mount Rushmore dedications. In spite of the remote location and the lack of good roads, 3,000 people came to Mount Rushmore.

With South Dakota now bursting with excitement, Borglum settled into the work of making a plan, one that reflected the country's struggles and successes. By the 1920s America had achieved much greatness with equal amounts of shame and pain. While American pioneers had established freedom from European rule and settled the west, they had treated the Native Americans brutally. Although the nation was now unified, it was scarred by the wounds of a civil war among its own people. In spite of the great industrialization that began during the late 19th century, World War I brought sharp attention to America's need to protect and assert its world power. Gutzon Borglum was profoundly influenced by these events—having witnessed them either through his immigrant parents or in his own life. With that perspective, it is no surprise that he would ultimately propose to carve the leaders he believed to be most instrumental in the glory of American democracy.

George Washington was born in 1732 in Virginia. He took school seriously, and learned the importance of courteous, reserved, dignified behavior. He never had any political aspirations, and focused on his trade of land surveyor until 1752, when he was appointed adjutant general of Virginia. From there he moved up in the army, serving under British General Braddock in the wars against the French and Indians. The general did not listen to young Washington about how to fight the Indians, and died at the battle of Fort Duquesne in 1755.

Washington later became the commander-in-chief of Virginia's frontier forces. After marrying in 1758, he resigned from the army. He planned to spend the rest of his life farming at Mount Vernon. But in 1770 he was appointed to a series of public jobs. He eventually became Commander-in-Chief of the Army of the United Colonies. He then spent eight years building an army in the hope of ridding his country of British domination.

After the success of the Revolutionary War, he again tried to go home to private life. But in 1787 he was invited to the Constitutional Convention, where he was immediately elected president. After the U.S. Constitution was adopted, Washington was elected the first president of the United States. He was elected to a second term in 1792. When his term ended in 1796, he retired to his home in Mount Vernon. He died in 1799.

Thomas Jefferson's life was rich with interesting accomplishments. He was a writer, mathematician, architect, lawyer, farmer, horse fancier, musician, educator, inventor, statesman, and patriot. Jefferson was born in Albemarle, Virginia, in April 1743, the third child and eldest son of 10 children. After attending William and Mary College, he was admitted to the Virginia Bar of Law in 1767.

Jefferson's involvement in politics began two years later when he was elected to the Virginia House of Burgesses. Eventually he was elected to the Continental Congress, during which he drafted the Declaration of Independence. Jefferson later resigned from Congress to return to Virginia to reform state laws. He became governor of the state in 1779.

By 1783 Jefferson returned to the federal government. He was elected to the U.S. Congress, served as minister to France, and became the country's third president at age 57. As president from 1801 to 1809, he was an advocate of westward expansion of the country. He arranged for the purchase of the Louisiana territory, a large region west of the Mississippi River, from France, then sent Lewis and Clark to explore this country.

After leaving the presidency, Jefferson founded the University of Virginia. He died in 1826 at age 83.

He proposed a memorial that would symbolize the country's founding, growth, preservation and development. He selected the images of the four presidents who led us through those key events that shaped the nation. They were George Washington, Thomas Jefferson, Abraham Lincoln, and Theodore Roosevelt.

No one objected to George Washington's representing "founding" of the nation. Nor did anyone object to the choice of Jefferson for "growth," as the country's size had doubled during his presidency through the Louisiana Purchase. In addition, Jefferson's writing of the Declaration of Independence certainly shaped the growth of the country's spirit and philosophy. Borglum's favorite choice was Abraham Lincoln, who represented "preservation" because of his ability to keep the nation unified in spite of a Civil War.

Borglum's last choice was the most *controversial*. Theodore Roosevelt was a personal friend of Borglum's. The fact that he had been a recent president and had only died in 1919 made the choice open to much discussion. Some women wanted Susan B. Anthony, a famous women's leader, to be the fourth figure. Several other choices were suggested and discussed.

But Borglum argued that Roosevelt represented "development." As president, he had opened up the national industrial growth to world trade by building the Panama Canal. At the same time, he protected the rights of workers. Senator Norbeck agreed. Before long, Roosevelt was the fourth and final figure to be included on Mount Rushmore. The four Presidents represent the first 150 years of democracy in the United States.

Next, Borglum switched his focus to the mechanics of actually carving on a mountain. In Georgia, he had been carving a "relief" of General Lee, removing the background stone so that the image of the men and horses would be raised from a stone background. But for Mount Rushmore, he wanted a more powerful result. Sculpting "in the round" was his objective so that each figure would stand on its own, against the sky. How he would

Abraham Lincoln was born in a log cabin near Hodgenville, Kentucky, in 1809. At 19 he traveled down the Mississippi River to New Orleans on a flat–bottomed cargo boat. At 21 he was doing physical labor in central

Illinois. Later he made a living splitting logs for rail fences. When he became a clerk in a store, and later the village post-master and deputy to the coun-ty surveyor, he began studying grammar and law. Lincoln read anything he could get his hands on, and became a very capable country lawyer.

In 1858 Lincoln ran for the U.S. Senate. Although he lost, he became nationally known because of debates with his opponent, Stephen Douglas. Two years later, he was elected the 16th president of the United States.

Before Lincoln was sworn in, many of the southern states decided to form their own country, the Confederate States of America. Lincoln, who had excel-lent instincts on military strategy, worked hard to bring an end to the Civil War without dissolving the Union. He was ultimately successful. In April 1865, as the war was ending, Lincoln was shot and killed by John Wilkes Booth. However, Lincoln's commitment to restore and secure a permanent union and to end slavery changed the United States forever.

In October 1858, Theodore Roosevelt was born into a wealthy New York City family. Educated by private tutors and widely traveled, he graduated from Harvard and attended Columbia Law School. He served in the New York State Legislature between the ages of 23 and 26. After the deaths of his mother and wife on the same day, he left New York for North Dakota, where he bought a farm.

Roosevelt returned to politics in 1886 by running for mayor. Although he was not elected, this led to many political appointments. In 1898, Roosevelt joined the military to fight in the Spanish-American War. He led his own regiment, called the Rough Riders, during the battle of San Juan Hill.

After returning home, Roosevelt became governor of New York State in 1899. He then became the running mate for William McKinley, who won the presidency in 1900. When McKinley was assassinated in September 1901, Roosevelt became the 26th president. He was popular, and was elected to a full term in 1904. As President, Roosevelt took an active role in world affairs. He started construction of the Panama Canal, and won the 1906 Nobel Peace Prize for helping to end a war beetween Russia and Japan. Roosevelt also supported progressive causes such as conservation and business reform. He died in 1919 at age 61.

do this was yet unknown to him or anyone else. Also, Borglum, Norbeck, and the other supporters faced another problem: finding enough money to pay for the immense project.

The head of Thomas Jefferson begins to emerge from the rock of Mount Rushmore. It took many years of careful work to create the enormous images in the granite face.

SELLING THE DREAM

Gutzon Borglum was not a man to rest on his *laurels*. Even though he was already famous for his painting and sculpture and had a loving wife and two healthy children, he was always restless, always seeking the next artistic challenge, political battle, or philosophical war. Now, at 58, he could see that all of his experiences in life had prepared him for this one, final challenge: creating Mount Rushmore. So what does one do when the dream is clear but the pathway is not *financed*? Borglum was sure private donations would fly in the door once it was known that he was behind the project, but that did not happen. Even with a roughed-out model, there was no money to begin the project. By 1927, hope sprang up when President Coolidge chose to spend his summer vacation in the Black Hills. During his stay, Senator Norbeck and Borglum did everything they could to win the president's attention and commitment to participate in a formal dedication of Mount Rushmore. They believed a presidential *endorsement* would open up people's wallets for financing the mountain carving. Their pressure paid off. On August 10 President Calvin Coolidge, dressed in cowboy boots and a 10-gallon hat, road a horse to the mountain's base. There, the crowd of nearly 3,000 heard an impassioned speech from Coolidge:

> The people of the future will see history and art combined to portray the spirit of patriotism. . . . This memorial will be another national shrine to which future generations will [go] to declare their continuing allegiance to independence, to self-government, to freedom and to economic justice.

Borglum, now 60 years old, was then lowered down the rock face in a swing seat to ceremoniously drill the first four holes in the mountainside. The work had officially begun! Coolidge's presence generated national publicity that prompted donations from several private sources, including $5,000 from Charles E. Rushmore, the man for whom the mountain was named. With $54,000 in hand, and the donation of a large diesel generator and two air compressors, work sheds and rough steps were built up the mountainside and 16 men were hired to begin work on October 4. By December, however, the operations closed for the winter, and no work was done at all in 1928.

Behind the scenes, Senator Norbeck and Representative Willamson continued to work hard to generate federal funds for Mount Rushmore. In 1929

Frank Lloyd Wright, the innovative and famous architect, saw Mount Rushmore as it was being carved and said, "The noble countenance emerges from Rushmore as though the spirit of the mountain had heard the human prayer and itself became a human countenance."

they succeeded with the passage of Public Law 805 and the creation of the Mount Rushmore Memorial Commission. This made $250,000 available for *matching funds*. The original $54,000 was immediately matched and work resumed. But by the end of 1929, a financial crash in the stock market brought all funding to a halt.

In 1931, the head of Jefferson was being carved into the mountain to the right of Washington's head when faulty rock was encountered. So the unfinished sculpture was blasted off the mountain and the new head was begun on Washington's left side, where it stands today.

That dark October day began a long era of the *Great Depression* in the United States, and few people had any extra money to give. With only $5,000 in the Rushmore treasury, it was now time to get creative. Borglum decided to create a brochure about Mount Rushmore that was filled with paid advertising; it generated $10,000 that was

In this 1929 photo, the face of George Washington emerges from the side of Mount Rushmore. Washington was the first portion of the sculpture to be finished; it was dedicated on July 4, 1930.

matched by the government fund. They also created a memorial membership club that generated $5,600, which was also matched. By spring of 1930, with more than $35,000 in the bank, the work was able to resume and continued up to the dedication of the George Washington figure on July 4.

Dedications had one main purpose: to generate publicity for interest, support, and funding. And Borglum knew how to make them special and attractive to the press and public alike. About 2,500 people attended the dedication of the George Washington face. They watched the rolling up of an enormous flag to reveal the partially completed face. The spectacle was accompanied by rifle salutes, a plane fly-by, and speeches. The event renewed the public's enthusiasm. Tourism to the site continued to increase every year, as people came to witness the men carving the mountain with dynamite. But after the crowds left on that July 4, the funding soon dried up again.

In February 1931, Borglum requested that the wealthy members of the memorial commission dig into their own pockets to contribute. They collected $18,000 dollars among them, which was matched by the government funds, and the work resumed. But in 1932, lack of funds shut down the operations again. This cycle of start and stop was repeated often over the 14-$\frac{1}{2}$ years of the project. Had the project been fully funded, it is estimated that the monument would have been completed in only 6-$\frac{1}{2}$ years.

In 1933, with many people out of work and hungry, the government was creating jobs by funding many large-scale projects, such as the building of roads, dams, and monuments. One of those roads was through the mountain leading to Mount

As a teenager, Lincoln Borglum, the sculptor's son, was asked to drive the first model of Mount Rushmore from Texas to South Dakota on his summer vacation. Unfortunately, he fell asleep at the wheel, and the car rolled over in a ditch. The base of the model broke, but not any of the sculpted heads. Lincoln was fine too, but his father was mighty angry at having to fix his model and his car!

In 1934 President Franklin D. Roosevelt signed a bill allowing federal funds to be spent on the Mount Rushmore project. With government money, the project moved toward completion. Roosevelt, who served as president from 1933 until his death in April 1945, was related to Theodore Roosevelt. FDR, as he was known, also approved funds for a memorial to Thomas Jefferson, which was built in Washington, D.C.

Rushmore. In 1934, President Franklin D. Roosevelt agreed that Mount Rushmore funding should not be limited to matching private funds. So the law was changed, and Mount Rushmore received direct government funding for the years ahead. That change gave the project a momentum and energy that resulted in the Thomas Jefferson face being dedicated in 1936 with 3,000 people attending. A year later, 1937, Lincoln's image was dedicated, with 5,000 people attending. And finally, in 1939, the dedication of Roosevelt's face brought 12,000 people to the mountain. This dedication was held at night, under a bright moon. Along with speeches, a ceremony by a Sioux Indian in full native dress, and visits by current-day movie celebrities, the crowd witnessed the explosions of brilliant rockets and aerial bombs before the powerful searchlights revealed the nearly finished heads of the four great presidents.

In 1941, the final appropriation for $86,000 was awarded to Mount Rushmore. For 14 years, Congress had endured the incessant and unstoppable badgering from Borglum not only for funding, but also for land, roads, and development of the monument's site so that his vision would be properly positioned and preserved. If time and money were infinite, Borglum might still be carving the mountain today. But World War II had begun in Europe, and it was commanding all the attention of the nation's government and its people.

While Gutzon Borglum did not live to see it, 1941 would be the last year of carving on Mount Rushmore. Borglum died in March of that year. His son Lincoln continued working, finishing the monument to its current form. The monument's carving operations were shut down on October 1, 1941.

A worker uses a powerful drill to punch holes into the granite face of Mount Rushmore. Honeycomb drilling made it easier to blast off sections of stone and shape the mountain. The finished dimensions of the Mount Rushmore faces are astonishing. Roosevelt's mustache is 20 feet long. Washington's mouth is 18 feet wide. Lincoln's mole is 16 inches across.

THE MUSCLE BEHIND THE MAGIC

*H*ow do you carve a 60-foot-high face on top of a mountain? Sculpting begins with study and reflection. Borglum studied photographs, portraits, sculptures, and descriptions of the presidents. He then used plaster and the tools of light and shadow to create faces that would have human character and vitality. His first *scale models* were small enough to be transported by car from his studio in Texas to the mountain site for viewing by the other leaders behind the project. The original design was a cluster of the four heads, but the granite on the mountain was unsuitable for that config-uration. Over the years, the model had to be changed

In the 1950s, filmmaker Alfred Hitchcock used Mount Rushmore as a location for his film *North by Northwest*. The film features a suspense-filled climax, in which the hero and heroine climb down the faces. They do this to escape their pursuers, but a stunt like this would be virtually impossible in reality.

nine times because of cracks and uncarvable rock.

After the design was approved, Borglum moved to a larger-scale working model that would have measurements that could be transferred to the mountain-sized carvings. One inch of the model equalled one foot of the finished mountain sculpture. That measurement was the single most important detail for being able to sculpt the granite rock. Unlike creating a "relief" sculpture, where Borglum could project the image he wanted onto the mountainside and simply carve away the unwanted rock around it, here he had to use a different technique to create an in-the-round sculpture. He invented a special pointer to transfer accurate measurements from model to mountain.

Sculptors have often said that they do not create a sculpture but simply reveal it. They explain that they "see" the image in the block of marble, wood, or stone, and simply carve away all the excess material around it. So how do you remove 450,000 tons of stone from a mountaintop to reveal a president's face? You carve with dynamite!

The process began with drillers using jackhammers to

make eight-foot-deep holes, two feet apart. Powdermen then placed sticks of dynamite, connected with blasting caps, into the holes and packed them with wet sand to keep the blast from getting too big. Every day at noon and four o'clock, the men left the mountain. Then there was a "blow-off" to send another layer of stone crashing down the mountainside.

Both the drillers and the powdermen navigated the massive mountain in swing seats. These were leather covered, steel-framed seats with side and waist straps for safety, with long straps connected to a winch on top of the mountain. Each chair was raised and lowered as needed for drilling and dynamite packing. At busy times the mountaintop used many people for very specific jobs. Winchmen lowered and raised the seats. Callboys were stationed to watch the workers and tell the winchmen which seats needed to be moved. Steelmen would swing new drill bits to the drillers, who had to change their bits every three feet of drilling. The blacksmith at the bottom of the hill would sharpen, on average, 400 drill bits a day.

The drilling and blasting took off 90 percent of the rock from the sculpture, leaving two to three inches for the artistic carving that gave each figure its life and vitality. That's when scaffolding was put up. It was attached to the rock face so the stone could be *honeycomb drilled* and hand chipped. Once the face was formed to the artist's satisfaction, the final step of bumping, with a *pneumatic drill* and special bit, finished the surface to the smoothness of a poured concrete sidewalk.

It was the attention to detail that gave the sculptures their life-like quality. After the majority of stone was removed, Borglum would study each face at different angles and in all kinds of light and shadow to determine what needed correction and adjustment. For example, the pupils in each president's eyes are shallow recessions with a long projecting shaft of granite. From a distance,

Each year thousands of people visit Mount Rushmore, which is a National Park.

however, that shaft catches the light and makes the eyes sparkle and look life-filled. Another example is the positioning of the heads themselves, such as when Borglum decided that Washington's head needed to be turned 20 degrees further south to have sun shining on it longer. There were thousands of adjustments as the work progressed over the 14 years. During the final finishing, Borglum would be lowered down in a harness to mark with red paint the features he wanted to emphasize or lines that needed softening. Then drillers would take three to four days to make those corrections. It took time, patience, and dedication.

While there were no government safety standards to follow in those days, Borglum was a tough self-regulator. Safety belts on the harnesses were never unstrapped until the worker's feet were safely on top of the mountain. Cables were checked daily and any excess wear was cut out. The chairs were staggered on the mountaintop to avoid anyone getting hit by a falling tool or rock. Scaffolding planks were constructed close together so tools or stone chips would not fall through. Masks and goggles were issued to avoid problems with granite dust. As a result of all of these measures, there were only a few minor injuries during the construction of Mount Rushmore. That is a very impressive record for any construction site!

After Gutzon Borglum passed away in March 1941, his son Lincoln took over the operations for its last seven months. Lincoln had worked full-time on the project since 1938 and knew what it took to make Mount Rushmore come alive. Lincoln may have led the workers up the 760 stairs each day at 7:30 A.M. and down again at 4:00, but he alone checked each face for the final time on that last day in October. He did so by bouncing across the faces in a swing chair, as if to say farewell and thank you to the stone that made his father's dream a gift to all mankind.

1789 George Washington is inaugurated as the first president of the United States; he serves as president until 1797.

1801 Thomas Jefferson becomes the third president of the United States; during his two terms in office a large tract of land west of the Mississippi River is purchased from France, more than doubling the size of the nation.

1861 Abraham Lincoln is sworn in a the nation's 16th president; during the next four years he attempts to preserve the union by waging the Civil War; after the surrender of the rebellious Southern states in April 1865, Lincoln is assassinated by John Wilkes Booth on April 14.

1901 Theodore Roosevelt becomes the 26th president after the death of President William McKinley on September 14. During his term, Roosevelt's accomplishments include construction of the Panama Canal and a peace agreement between Japan and Russia, for which he wins the 1906 Nobel Peace Prize.

1923 Doane Robinson proposes building a gigantic monument on the Needles in the Black Hills to encourage tourism to South Dakota.

1924 Sculptor Gutzon Borglum is invited to study the proposal. He decided the Needles is not the right location and suggests that the sculpture should reflect national, not regional, heroes.

1925 Borglum visits again and selects Mount Rushmore and accepts project; dedication ceremony held at mountain site; fundraising begins.

1926 Rough models of monument built with Washington, Jefferson, Lincoln and Roosevelt.

1927 Dedication on August 10; President Coolidge calls Mount Rushmore a "national shrine" and pledges national funds.

1928 Money runs out and work stops.

1929 Congress passes Public Law 805, authorizing matching funds of $250,000.

1930 Washington's face unveiled and dedicated.

1932 Money runs out, and work stops on the monument; South Dakota receives $100,000 in federal grants for road building project, including one to Mount Rushmore.

1934 Matching fund law amended to provide direct funding to memorial.

1935 Congress authorizes $200,000 to complete Mount Rushmore.

1936 The image of Thomas Jefferson is dedicated, in a ceremony attended by President Franklin Roosevelt.

1937 Abraham Lincoln's image is dedicated.

1938 Congress authorizes $300,000; Lincoln Borglum supervises project.

1939 Theodore Roosevelt's image is dedicated; Congress imposes a deadline of June 1940 to complete Mount Rushmore.

1940 Congress authorizes final grant of $86,000.

1941 Gutzon Borglum dies in March at age 72; Lincoln Borglum continues work on the monument for seven more months; on October 1 funding ends.

1991 The 50th anniversary of Mount Rushmore is celebrated with a final dedication ceremony involving President George H. Bush.

commission—a contract to produce a product in exchange for a fee.

controversy—a disagreement or arguement caused by some idea or action.

endorsement—to publicly express approval or support of a project or a person.

finance—to acquire the money needed to proceed with a project.

Great Depression—a time of high unemployment and hard times in the United States. It began with the stock market crash of 1929 and lasted until the late 1930s.

honeycomb drilling—a process of drilling small holes, close together, in the granite so that a chisel and hammer could easily wedge off the unwanted rock. After drilling and before chipping, the rock looked like a bee's honeycomb.

laurels—a reference to a symbol of fame and honor, presented by the Greeks as a wreath of bay leaves. "Resting on one's laurels" means not working hard because of one's past success.

mass-production—a process for making large quantities of an item that are then usually sold; such as a factory for making cars.

matching funds—a typical contribution method where one donor (such as the government) agrees to give money in equal amount to private donations.

pneumatic drill—a powerful drill that works using compressed air or gas.

prosperity—a time of success and good fortune.

scale model—a smaller version of any construction, such as a building or a sculpture, so that it can be viewed, evaluated, and adjusted prior to its full-size construction.

FURTHER READING

Borglum, Lincoln. *Mount Rushmore: The Story Behind the Scenery.* Las Vegas: KC Publications, 1993.

Curley, Lynn. *Rushmore.* New York: Scholastic Press, 1999.

Presnall, Judith Janda. *Mount Rushmore.* San Diego: Lucent Books, 2000.

Shaff, Howard, and Audrey Karl Shaff. *Six Wars At A Time.* Connecticut: Permedia Publishing, 1985.

Smith, Rex Alan. *The Carving of Mount Rushmore.* New York: Abbeville Press, Inc., 1985.

St. George, Judith. *The Mount Rushmore Story.* New York: G.P. Putnam's Sons, 1985.

INTERNET RESOURCES

National Park Service
http://www.nps.gov/moru/

Visiting South Dakota
http://www.travelsd.com/

Mount Rushmore History
http://www.mtrushmore.net/
http://www.pbs.org/wgbh/amex/rushmore/
http://www.americanparknetwork.com/parkinfo/ru/history/carve.html

PICTURE CREDITS

page

3: National Park Service photo/Mount Rushmore National Memorial

8: James L. Amos/Corbis

12: Hulton/Archive

14: Rise Studio, Rapid City, South Dakota/Mount Rushmore National Memorial

17: Underwood & Underwood/Corbis

20: Charles E. Rotkin/Corbis

23: Independence National Historic Park, Philadelphia

24: National Portrait Gallery, Smithsonian Institution/ Art Resource, NY

26: National Portrait Gallery, Smithsonian Institution/ Art Resource, NY

27: National Portrait Gallery, Smithsonian Institution/ Art Resource, NY

28: Underwood & Underwood/Corbis

32: Hulton/Archive

34: Bettmann/Corbis

36: Lincoln Borglum/Mount Rushmore National Memorial

40: Kevin Eilbeck/Mount Rushmore National Memorial

Cover photos: Charles E. Rotkin/Corbis; (inset) Underwood & Underwood/Corbis; (back) National Park Service photo/Mount Rushmore National Memorial

BARRY MORENO has been librarian and historian at the Ellis Island Immigration Museum and the Statue of Liberty National Monument since 1988. He is the author of *The Statue of Liberty Encyclopedia*, which was published by Simon and Schuster in October 2000. He is a native of Los Angeles, California. After graduation from California State University at Los Angeles, where he earned a degree in history, he joined the National Park Service as a seasonal park ranger at the Statue of Liberty; he eventually became the monument's librarian. In his spare time, Barry enjoys reading, writing, and studying foreign languages and grammar. His biography has been included in *Who's Who Among Hispanic Americans*, *The Directory of National Park Service Historians*, *Who's Who in America*, and *The Directory of American Scholars*.

LAURA HAHN is a creative writing teacher for young people and a freelance writer of articles, stories, plays, and business copy. Earlier in her career she worked as a professional writer and communicator for corporations. Her most satisfying work is focused on creating understanding of how human beings do what they do, especially when it comes to making a difference and following their bliss.